Homophones
at Home

By Kathleen Connors

Gareth Stevens

Please visit our website, www.garethstevens.com. For a free color catalog of all our high-quality books, call toll free 1-800-542-2595 or fax 1-877-542-2596.

Library of Congress Cataloging-in-Publication Data

Connors, Kathleen.
Homophones at home / Kathleen Connors.
    p. cm. — (Word play)
Includes index.
ISBN 978-1-4339-7188-4 (pbk.)
ISBN 978-1-4339-7189-1 (6-pack)
ISBN 978-1-4339-7187-7 (library binding)
1. English language—Homonyms—Juvenile literature. I. Title.
PE1595.C59 2012
428.1—dc23

                                2011051767

First Edition

Published in 2013 by
Gareth Stevens Publishing
111 East 14th Street, Suite 349
New York, NY 10003

Copyright © 2013 Gareth Stevens Publishing

Designer: Andrea Davison-Bartolotta
Editor: Kristen Rajczak

Photo credits: Cover, p. 1 (main image) Szekeres Szabolcs/Shutterstock.com; cover, p. 1 (magnets) Elena Schweitzer/Shutterstock.com; p. 5 JupiterImages/Comstock/Thinkstock; p. 7 © iStockphoto.com/Rhienna Cutler; p. 9 Rossario/Shutterstock.com; p. 11 Comstock Images/Thinkstock; p. 13 JupiterImages/Brand X Pictures/Thinkstock; p. 15 Digital Vision/Getty Images; p. 17 Digital Vision/Photodisc/Thinkstock; p. 19 Sonya Etchison/Shutterstock.com; p. 20 iStockphoto/Thinkstock.

Printed in the United States of America

CPSIA compliance information: Batch #CS12GS: For further information contact Gareth Stevens, New York, New York at 1-800-542-2595.

Contents

Boldface words appear in the glossary.

Finding Homophones

Do you **know** what a homophone is? If you said **no**, then you're about to find out!

Homophones are words that sound the same but are spelled differently. Say **know** and **no** out loud. They sound the same!

Let's look for more homophones around your house.

Keeping Warm

When it's **chilly** outside, you can eat **chili** to warm up.

Chilly and **chili** show that while homophones sound the same, they have different **meanings**. **Chilly** is another way of saying cold. **Chili** is a thick soup often made with tomatoes, beans, and meat.

Tummy Trouble

Your little brother told you he **ate eight** cookies after dinner. He's going to have a **stomachache**!

Say **ate** and **eight** out loud. Do they sound the same? **Ate** and **eight** are homophones.

Welcome!

It's important to be kind to a **guest**. Have you **guessed** what a **guest** is? A **guest** is someone who visits your house.

Guest and **guessed** are homophones. They sound the same but don't have the same meaning.

Telling Time

Check the clock! An **hour** before **our** bedtime, we take a bath and read a story.

Hour and **our** are homophones. They sound the same but have different meanings.

Fruity Fun

Many families put a fruit bowl out in their kitchen. It might hold a **pair** of bananas, oranges, an apple, or a **pear**.

A **pair** is two of something. A **pear** is a kind of fruit. **Pair** and **pear** are homophones!

Good Smells

Use **flour** to help bake muffins, or pick a **flower** to give your grandma. Both will make her smile!

Do you think **flour** and **flower** are homophones? Say them out loud to be sure!

Three of a Kind

Some homophones come in threes!

Two days a week, you have **chores to** do. You clean your room and walk the dog. You set the table every day, **too**.

Two, **to**, and **too** all sound the same. They're homophones.

Home Sweet Home

Sometimes, just staying at home is fun! If you get **bored**, you can play a **board** game or play in the yard.

Say **bored** and **board** out loud. Do they sound the same? They're homophones!

Common Homophones

bee		be
deer		dear
bye	by	buy
eye		I
knew		new
see		sea

Glossary

chore: a job you do around the house

meaning: the message behind a word or words

stomachache: a pain in your stomach

For More Information

Books

Barretta, Gene. *Dear Deer: A Book of Homophones.* New York, NY: Henry Holt and Company, 2007.

Coffelt, Nancy. *Aunt Ant Leaves Through the Leaves: A Story with Homophones and Homonyms.* New York, NY: Holiday House, 2011.

Websites

Homophones Video
pbskids.org/video/?category=Between%20the%20Lions&pid=jlxn0U PSPVhu8rltZelQOprWACkv_V5W
Watch a video and hear a song about homophones.

Pairs Word Game
www.learninggamesforkids.com/vocabulary-games/homophones-games/homophones.html
Learn more homophone pairs and practice using them correctly.

Publisher's note to educators and parents: Our editors have carefully reviewed these websites to ensure that they are suitable for students. Many websites change frequently, however, and we cannot guarantee that a site's future contents will continue to meet our high standards of quality and educational value. Be advised that students should be closely supervised whenever they access the Internet.

Index